MW00666975

THE FIDDLE CLUB

FIDDLE TUNES FOR THE BEGINNING TO INTERMEDIATE VIOLINIST

COLLECTION 2

SWATH PUBLISHING MEL BAY®

1 2 3 4 5 6 7 8 9 0

The Fiddle Club – Collection 2
Fourth Edition

International Standard Music Number
M-706020-02-0

EM – 2

Printed in Canada

Published by:

Swath Publishing
Box 758, Suite 105
150 Crowfoot Cresc. NW
Calgary, AB
T3G 3T2
Ph. (403) 208-4040
Fx. (403) 208-4042
Web: www.barrage.org

Preface

It was never planned – it was just one of those things that just seemed to evolve. As fiddle players and music instructors, we were constantly asked to write out fiddle tunes. The Fiddle Club series was our response to these requests. It is our hope that the books and recordings in this expanding series will serve as a valuable resource to anyone interested in this style of music.

As you play through the music in this book, we want to remind you that the tunes should not necessarily be considered the original or correct versions. You can literally find hundreds of variations of the same tune. The settings found in this book are simply our interpretation.

We have included various markings (bar numbers, fingerings, and bowings) which we have found helpful in teaching – especially in group situations. As always, experienced players may want to alter some of these markings and add their own dynamics to reflect their personal style.

Traditionally, fiddling has been an improvised aural art form which makes it very difficult to notate. We recommend that you take every opportunity to listen, watch and play with other fiddlers.

The tunes in this book have been recorded and are available on CD. In the recording, you will notice that the tunes have been grouped into medleys which follow the order of the book. You may want to experiment with different groupings. For those individuals who would like to perform this material, piano and guitar accompaniments are available.

Keep your eye out for future collections and keep fiddling!

Yours sincerely,

Dean Marshall

A native Albertan, Dean Marshall is well-known for his performing, arranging, composing and teaching skills.

Dean received his early musical training at the Mount Royal College Conservatory, where he completed an AMRC, ARCT and a music performance diploma. In 1985, he went on to obtain a Bachelor of Music Performance degree at the University of Toronto. While completing his studies, Dean earned numerous awards and accolades. In particular, he was a first prize winner at the Grand North American Fiddle Championships, nominated Instrumentalist of the Year by the CCMA and won first place in the Calgary Stampede talent competition.

Dean's interest in arranging and composing has resulted in many exciting and successful projects. His arrangements have been performed by the Calgary Philharmonic Orchestra under conductor Richard Hayman. Dean was also Artistic Director of The Calgary fiddlers for 8 years and produced several recordings for the group.

Currently, Dean is one of the creators and founders of Barrage, a contemporary, violin-based entertainment that has gained an international following. As Artistic Director of Barrage, Dean is dramatically expanding the violin repertoire and inspiring players and musical enthusiasts of all ages.

John Crozman

John Crozman was born in Cape Breton and grew up in London, Canada. Introduced to the violin at public school, John eventually went on to complete a Bachelor of Music degree in education at the University of Western Ontario. This was followed by postgraduate studies at the Guildhall School of Music in London, England. In the midst of his formal studies, John adopted the viola as his principal instrument.

The violin, however, was not neglected as he continued to explore his passion for fiddle music. He won several contests across Canada, including the Canadian Open Novelty Class (4 times) and has given numerous performances in England, Scotland, Germany, Canada and the United States. John has also performed on the CBC, CTV, BBC and Global Television Networks. In England, he had the honour of playing for violinist Yehudi Menuhin on the occasion of his 70th birthday.

John taught at the Mount Royal College Conservatory of Music for 7 years and is the former Managing Director of The Calgary Fiddlers. Currently, he is an integral part of the creative team responsible for the formation, development and management of Barrage. John's commitment to music education is realized through the international success of Barrage - a key component in John's exploration of the artistic possibilities of string instruments.

Contents

To the Ladies

Violin 1

Traditional

To the Ladies

Violin 2

Traditional

Haste to the Wedding

Violin 1

Traditional

Haste to the Wedding

Violin 2

Traditional

Moll in the Wad Jig

Traditional

Blue Water Hornpipe

(President Garfield's Hornpipe)

Traditional

Elliott's Favorite Reel

Traditional

This page left intentionally blank to facilitate page turns

Centennial Waltz

Violin 1

Traditional

Centennial Waltz

Violin 2

Traditional

Blackjack Whiskey

Violin 1

Graham Townsend
Arranged by Dean Marshall

Used by permission

Blackjack Whiskey (Continued)

Violin 1

Used by permission

Blackjack Whiskey

Violin 2

Graham Townsend
Arranged by Dean Marshall

Blackjack Whiskey (Continued)

Violin 2

Used by permission

This page left
intentionally
blank to facilitate
page turns

Cape Breton Jig

Traditional

Silver and Gold Two-Step

Violin 1

Traditional

Silver and Gold Two-Step

Violin 2

Traditional

Flannigan's Polka

Traditional

Violin 1

Flannigan's Polka

Traditional

Violin 2

Georgiana Moon

Traditional

Buttermilk Mary

Traditional

Minstrel's Fancy

Violin 1

Traditional

Minstrel's Fancy

Violin 2

Traditional

Woodchopper's Reel

Ned Landry

Carpenter's Reel

(Walker Street)

Traditional

Soldiers Joy

Violin 1

Traditional

Soldiers Joy

Violin 2

Traditional

Geese in the Bog

Traditional

Mason's Apron

Traditional

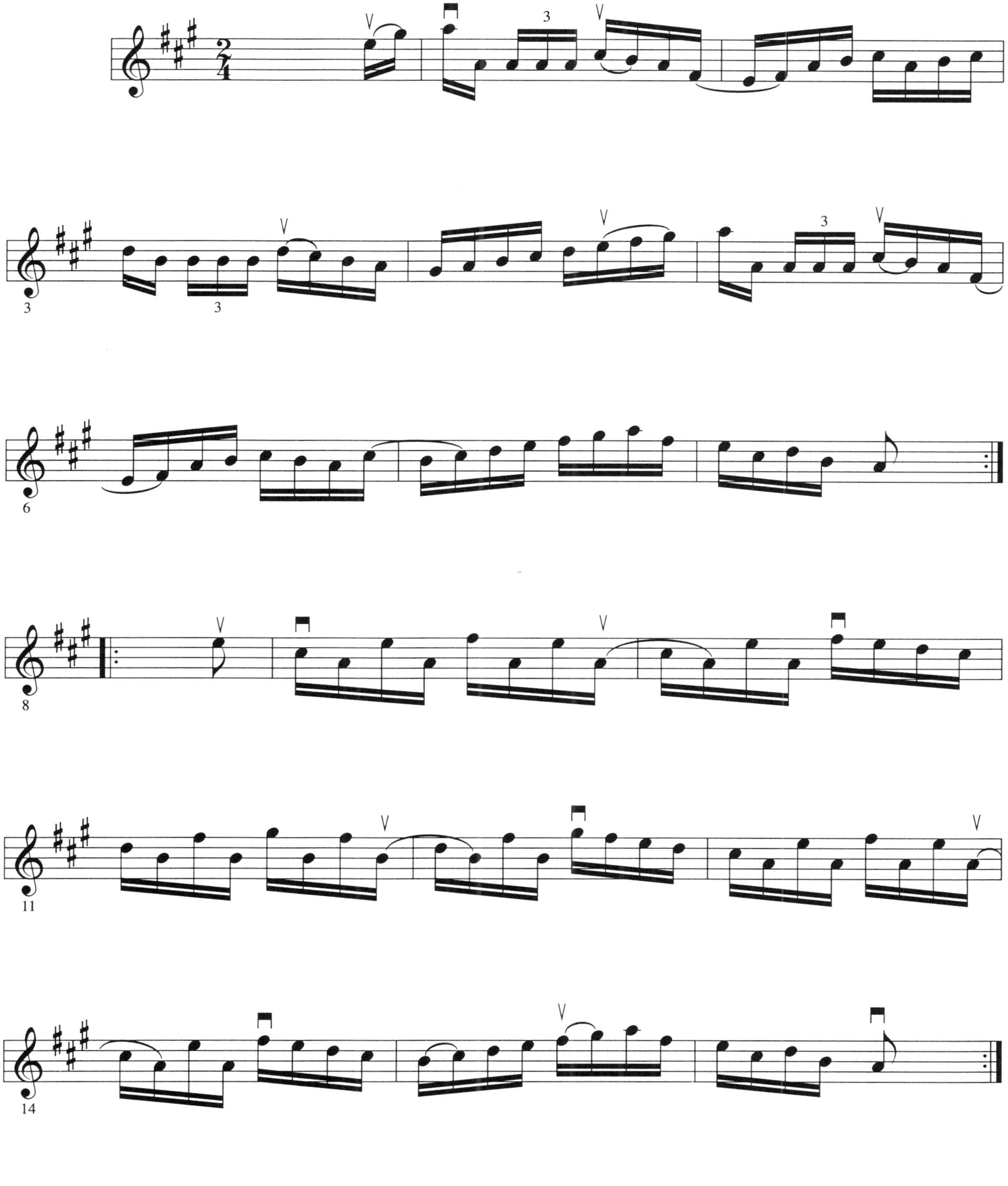

Rochester Schottische

Traditional

Rochester Schottische (Continued)

Donegal Jig

Traditional

Winding Stream

(Mrs Thorton's Reel)

Traditional

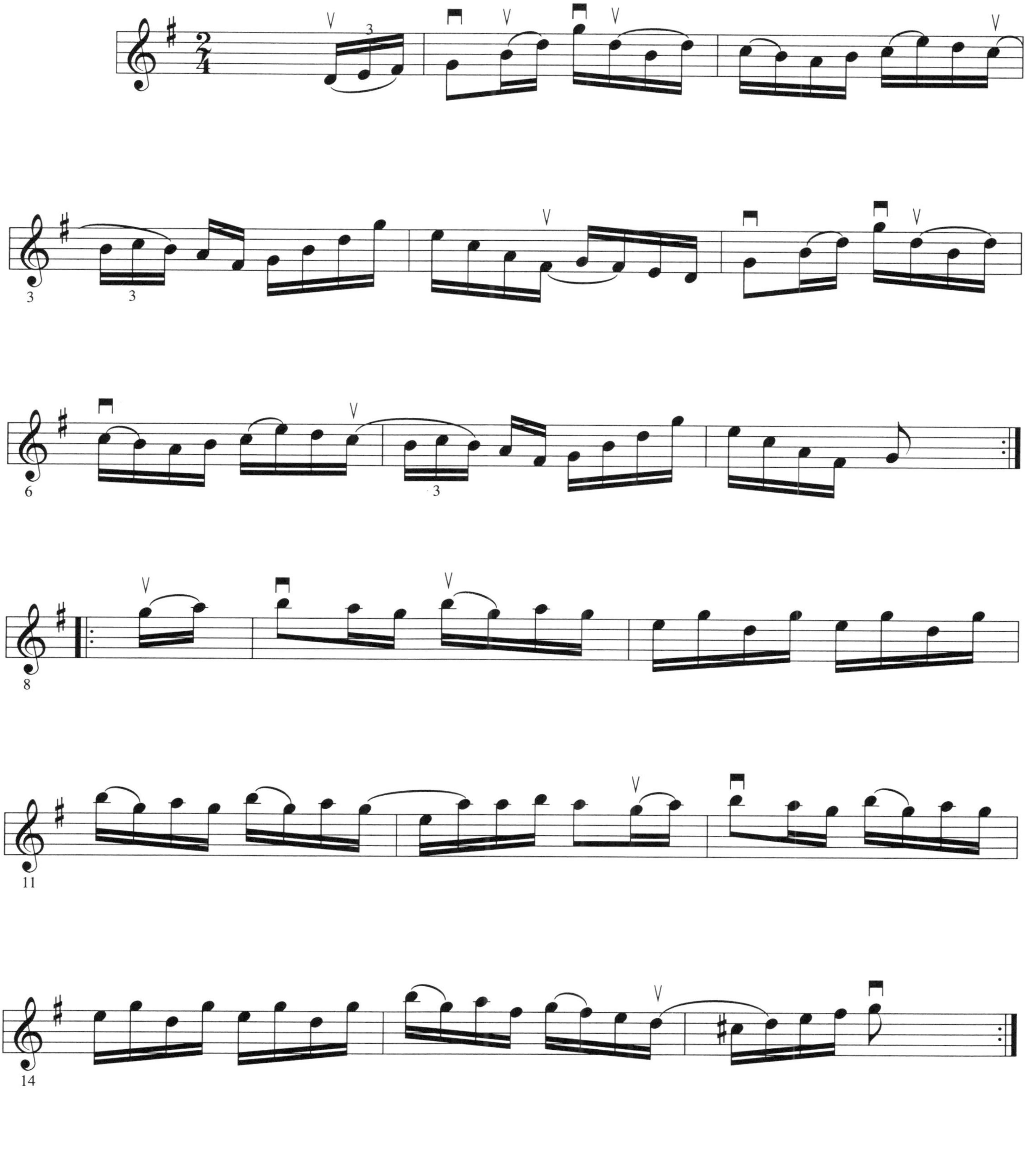

Patronella

Violin 1

Traditional

Patronella

Violin 2

Traditional

Rustic Jig

Traditional

Farmer's Jamboree

Traditional

Smash the Window

Traditional

Irish Washerwoman

Traditional

Red River Waltz

Andy De Jarlis

Westphalia Waltz

Traditional

Plaza Polka

Violin 1

Traditional

Plaza Polka

Violin 2

Traditional

Lady of the Lake

Traditional

Growlin' Old Man & Old Woman

Traditional

Crooked Stovepipe

Violin 1

Traditional

Crooked Stovepipe

Violin 2

Traditional

The Old Man And The Old Woman

Violin 1

Traditional

The Old Man And The Old Woman

Violin 2

Traditional

Anniversary Waltz

Violin 1

Traditional

Anniversary Waltz

Violin 2

Traditional

Fisher's Hornpipe

Violin 1

Traditional

Fisher's Hornpipe

Violin 2

Traditional

McDowell's Breakdown

Violin 1

Graham Townsend
Arranged by Dean Marshall

Used by permission

McDowell's Breakdown

Violin 2

Graham Townsend
Arranged by Dean Marshall

Used by permission

McDowell's Breakdown

Violin 3

Graham Townsend
Arranged by Dean Marshall

Notes